The Cats On My Block

written by Valerie Sicignano
illustrated by Jane Sayre Denny

100% of the profits from the sale of this book will go to The Humane Society of New York's Feral Cat Program.

© 2014, The Humane Society of New York

www.HumaneSocietyNY.org

Dedicated to my favorite person in the entire universe...

BL

Special thanks to Megan, a true friend to the cats of New York City

Somewhere in New York City...

LUKE: Look at those paw prints.

I wonder what animal made them?

WILLOW: The cats on my block made them.

Look, there's one now.

LUKE: Wow! Let's go out and pet them.

WILLOW: These cats are feral. They can't be petted or picked up.

WILLOW: Feral cats live outside.

LUKE: So they're homeless?

WILLOW: No. The outdoors **is** their home.

WILLOW: My neighbor Keith is their caregiver.

He gives the cats fresh food and water every morning and evening.

WILLOW: Keith is a good neighbor. After the cats have eaten

he cleans up so there is no mess left behind.

LUKE: Look! A litter of kittens!

KEITH: A mother cat showed up this morning
with her three babies.

When the kittens are old enough to get along without their mother
I will get her spayed at the veterinarian so there won't be any more
litters born.

There are too many cats and kittens already
and not enough indoor homes for all of them.

KEITH: This is called "Trap-Neuter-Return" or TNR for short.

It means that the cats are trapped – because they can't be picked up –

and taken to the veterinarian.

The vet will spay the females and neuter the males

so they cannot have more litters.

They will also get their vaccinations and a left eartip.

Next, they will rest and recover inside for several days.

Then they will be released exactly where they were trapped,

and the colony will be cared for every day by a caregiver like me.

Trap

+

Neuter

+

Return

LUKE: What will happen to the kittens?

KEITH: These kittens are young enough to be tamed.

I will socialize them and then find good people to adopt them

so they can live indoors.

LUKE: Why do the cats have one pointy ear and one flat ear?

KEITH: The flat ear is called an eartip. It is on the left ear. The veterinarian does this as a way to mark which cats have been spayed or neutered and had their vaccinations. The vet leaves the right ear pointy.

Can you tell which cat is the kittens' mother?

WILLOW: The white one...

LUKE: ...because she does **not** have a left eartip.

LUKE: Where do the cats go when it rains or snows?

WILLOW: Keith built shelters for the cats.

They go inside them when it rains or snows or gets really cold.

The shelters have straw insulation inside to keep

the cats warm and dry.

LUKE: Do the cats have names?
Do they have different personalities?

KEITH: Yes, all the cats have names
and each one has a different personality.
They have complex and caring relationships
with each other—just like people.
I know and **love** these cats even though
I cannot pet them or pick them up.

Meet the Cats!

The Cats:

Star

Sky

Comet

Cloud

Moon Dust

The Kittens:

Starry Night

Midnight

Moon Light

STAR...

7-year-old female.

Companion of Sky.

Mother of Comet and Cloud.

Favorite pastimes include

chasing butterflies

and rolling in the grass.

SKY...

7-year-old male.

Companion of Star.

Father of Comet and Cloud.

Loves music and visits from his children.

COMET...

6-year-old male.

Son of Star and Sky.

Brother of Cloud.

Knows his name and comes when called.

CLOUD...

6-year-old female.

Daughter of Star and Sky.

Sister of Comet.

Keeps a watchful eye on the new kittens.

MOON DUST...

Female, age unknown.

Mother of the 3 kittens.

Spends her time teaching her kittens

how to be independent.

Moon Dust's kittens spend their days playing and sleeping.

STARRY NIGHT...
6-week-old female.
She is curious about her
surroundings and all the
new cats and people
in her life.

MIDNIGHT...
6-week-old male.
He is outgoing
and likes to surprise
his siblings.

MOON LIGHT...
6-week-old female.
She is shy
and loves to nap
in the shelter.

LUKE: I'm so happy the cats have a caregiver to give them fresh food, clean water, a warm, dry shelter and love!

MEOW

(The End)

GLOSSARY OF

Caregiver: a person who looks after an outdoor feral cat colony and provides regular food, water and shelter.

Catology: the study of all things cat.

Colony: a group of cats living in one place.

Eartip: when a veterinarian removes a small part of the tip of the left ear of a feral cat to mark the cat as spayed or neutered and vaccinated when seen from a distance.

Feral Cat: a cat that has not been tamed. Feral cats prefer to live outdoors.

Litter: a group of kittens born to a cat at the same time. The kittens in a litter are siblings (brothers and sisters).

Neuter/Neutered: the surgery during which a veterinarian sterilizes a male cat so he can no longer reproduce (have kittens).

Paw Prints: the impressions or images left behind by the paws of cats and kittens. They can be indentations in the ground or images on the surface.

Shelter: a structure that covers or protects people, animals or things.

FERAL CATOLOGY

Socialize: the process of teaching a feral kitten how to interact with humans and live in an indoor home.

Spay/Spayed: the surgery during which a veterinarian sterilizes a female cat so she can no longer reproduce (have kittens).

Tame: the process of teaching a feral kitten how to interact with humans and live in an indoor home.

Trap-Neuter-Return (TNR): a process in which feral cats are humanely trapped, spayed or neutered, given a rabies vaccination, eartipped and returned to the outdoor location where they were found to be cared for daily by a caregiver.

Vaccinate/Vaccinations: to give an animal a vaccine to prevent infection by a disease.

Vet/Veterinarian: an animal doctor.

About the Illustrator

Jane Sayre Denny is an award-winning graphic designer & artist with a deep love of cats. She is the author and illustrator of *The Twelve Cats of Christmas, Emmaline*, and illustrator of the *Power Kid* series of child empowerment books by Obi Nwokolo.

Jane lives in Queens with her three indoor cats, Julie, Jack and Cindy, and cares for a colony of ten outdoors, very much like the cats in this book. Her cat family provides endless artistic inspiration.

Jane has rescued, lived with and loved many cats, but it was Crazy Johnny – the deaf, white, quirky kitten with the big voice – who inspired her perennial work and raison d'etre, *The Pride, the Award-Winning *Reality* Cat Cartoon.*

The Pride won the 2007 International Cat Writers' Association Muse Medallion for best cat cartoon. *The Twelve Cats of Christmas* (a feline retelling of the famous song, *The Twelve Days of Christmas*) won the Cat Writers' 2012 Certificate of Excellence, Muse Medallion, and the Kuykendall Image Award for outstanding image series featuring cats.

About the Author

Valerie Sicignano completed a Certificate in Humane Education at the ASPCA in 1997. In 2007, she was the Keynote Speaker at the United Federation of Teachers (UFT) Humane Education Conference in New York City, where she also wrote and presented a workshop for teachers. Her UFT Keynote Address focused on creating service learning projects that benefit people, animals and the environment.

The author in the 1970s

Also in 2007, Valerie produced the Humane Education Leadership Conference in New York City. She has presented humane education workshops for adults and children in New York City and Houston. Along with Kerry Lea, Valerie was the leader of a Jane Goodall Institute Roots & Shoots group called The Veg Kids, who performed original songs about the importance of helping animals and the environment at numerous venues, including the United Nations.

Valerie is a Cofounder of the New York City Feral Cat Initiative, a program of the Mayor's Alliance for NYC's Animals, which began in January 2005. In 2003, she was honored with the Animal Guardian Award from the *Manhattan Pet Gazette* and in 2006, she received the Companion Animal Guardian Award from In Defense of Animals.

Made in the USA
Columbia, SC
11 September 2020